Animal Tales and Legends

A Dolch Classic Basic Reading Book

by Edward W. Dolch and Marguerite P. Dolch

illustrated by Kersti Frigell

The Basic Reading Books

The Basic Reading Books are fun reading books that fill the need for easy-to-read stories for the primary grades. The interest appeal of these folktales and legends will encourage independent reading at the early reading levels.

The stories focus on the 95 Common Nouns and the Dolch 220 Basic Sight Vocabulary. Beyond these simple lists, the books use about two or three new words per page.

This series was prepared under the direction and supervision of Edward W. Dolch, Ph.D.

This revision was prepared under the direction and supervision of Eleanor Dolch LaRoy and the Dolch Family Trust.

SRA/McGraw-Hill

A Division of The **McGraw·Hill** *Companies*

Original version copyright © 1958 by Edward W. Dolch.
Copyright © 1999 by SRA/McGraw-Hill. All rights reserved.
Except as permitted under the United States Copyright Act, no part of this publication may be reproduced or distributed in any form or by any means, or stored in a database or retrieval system without prior written permission from the publisher.

Printed in the United States of America.

Send all inquiries to:
SRA/McGraw-Hill
250 Old Wilson Bridge Road, Suite 310
Worthington, OH 43085

ISBN 0-02-830812-3

1 2 3 4 5 6 7 8 9 0 BUX 04 03 02 01 00 99 98

Table of Contents

The Cat and the Mice

There was an old cat who lived in a farm house. And many mice lived in that farm house, too. For a long time the cat had as many mice to eat as she wanted.

But now that the cat was old. She could not jump or run so fast. There was many a time when the old cat did not have a mouse to eat.

The old cat said to herself, "I must do something about this."

And so the cat called all the mice together.

"We have lived in this farm house for a long, long time. But we have not been friends," said the cat. "And I have been thinking that if I were your friend and did not hurt you, you would be friends with me."

The mice did not know what to think of a cat who wanted to be friends with them.

"I will let you play all over the house," said the cat. "I will not hurt you. All I ask is that you be friends with me."

There were two mice who were brothers, Brother Ambe and Brother Rambe. They walked up to the old cat and said, "And what shall the mice do to show that they are friends with you?"

"Well," said the cat, "when the sun is going down, I will sit by the door. Every mouse in the farm house can walk before me. As you go before me, you can bow to me to show me that you are my friend."

The mice talked together. Then Brother Ambe and Brother Rambe walked up to the old cat.

"The mice wish to be friends with you," they said to the old cat. "When the sun is going down, the mice will walk before you and bow to you to show you that they are your friends."

From that time on, the mice played about the farm house and the cat did not hurt them. But when the sun was going down, the cat sat by the door and the mice walked before her. And as the last mouse bowed to the cat, the cat ate that mouse right up. And no one saw what the cat did.

One day Brother Ambe said to Brother Rambe, "Brother Rambe, there are not so many mice about the farm house. Where do you think they are?"

"Brother Ambe, I have been thinking that maybe the cat knows where the mice are," said Brother Rambe.

"Today, when we walk by the cat, I will be the first," said Brother Ambe. "And you, Brother Rambe, will be the last. I will call to you and you will answer me." And that is what they did.

When Ambe had bowed to the old cat, he called, "Brother Rambe, where are you?"

"Here I am," called Brother Rambe, who was the very last mouse. And so the cat did not get to eat the last mouse that day, because Brother Ambe called to Brother Rambe. And Brother Rambe answered.

The cat was hungry and she did not sleep well.

The next time when the mice walked before the cat, Brother Ambe was first again. And Brother Rambe was last again.

When Ambe had bowed to the old cat, he called, "Brother Rambe, where are you?"

"Here I am," called Brother Rambe, who was the very last mouse.

The old cat was hungry. She was very hungry. The old cat gave a big jump.

"RUN, RUN, RUN," called Brother Rambe. The mice ran away as fast as they could go.

The old cat did not get a mouse to eat, and never again did the mice try to be friends with a cat.

The Camel and the Pig

Once upon a time a camel and a pig were walking down the road together.

"It is better to be tall," said the camel to the pig. "I can put my head over a garden wall and eat all the good things that grow there in the garden."

"It is much better to be small," said the pig to the camel. "I can go in the smallest garden door and eat all the good things that grow there in the garden."

And so the camel and the pig talked and talked. Was it better to be tall? Was it better to be small? At last the camel said to the pig, "I know that it is better to be tall. And if you do not think so after we have had our walk together, I will give you the hump on my back."

The pig was not going to be outdone by the camel and so the pig said to the camel, "I know that it is better to be small and if you do not think so after we have had our walk together, I will give you my nose."

The camel and the pig walked on down the road together. Pretty soon they got to a garden. There was a wall around the garden, but there was no door in the wall.

The camel put his head over the wall and ate the good things in the garden. But there was no way that the pig could get into the garden.

"You can see that it is better to be tall," said the camel. "I can put my head over the wall and get all I want to eat, but you cannot get any of the good things in the garden."

The pig did not say anything. And so the camel and the pig walked on down the road. Pretty soon, they came to another garden with a wall around it. The wall was so high that the camel could not put his head over it.

But the pig found a little door, and into the garden he went. He ate all the good things in the garden that he wanted. When he came out of the garden, he found the camel by the wall.

Then the camel said to the pig, "Sometimes it is better to be tall. And sometimes it is better to be small."

"Right you are," said the pig. "And it is better for a camel to be tall."

"Right you are," said the camel. "And it is better for a pig to be small."

"You must keep your hump," said the pig to the camel. "I would not know what to do with a hump on my back."

"And my own nose is a good nose for me," said the camel. "You must keep your own nose, Pig."

And the camel and the pig walked on down the road together.

The Goat and the Wolf

Once upon a time there were seven goats who lived together on a farm. Every morning the farmer let the goats out, and they went up on the hills and ate grass. A big, black dog went with them. He looked after the goats.

At night the dog would bring the goats down from the hills. The goats went back to the farm and the farmer put them into the barn.

But one night one of the goats did not come down from the hills with the other goats. He went up the hill so that the dog could not find him. And he said to himself, "I have always wanted to sleep up in the hills all night. And so I will not go back to the farm tonight."

The goat was very glad to get away from the dog so that he could sleep up in the hills at night. But he did not see a hungry old wolf that had come to the hills looking for something to eat.

"Brother Goat," said the wolf, "what are you doing on my hills at night?"

Now the goat thought very fast and so he said to the wolf, "Brother Wolf, I was just looking for you. I wanted to thank you for the green grass that grows upon your hills."

"Don't you know that I like to eat goats?" said the wolf.

"Oh, yes," said the goat. "I know that you are going to eat me. But all this time I have been eating the green grass that grows on your hills. So it is only right that you should eat me."

The wolf thought that was a very funny thing for a goat to say. The goat when on, "Brother Wolf, I have one thing to ask of you before you eat me."

"And what is that?" asked the wolf.

"I want to sing before you eat me," said the goat.

"I did not know that goats could sing," said the wolf.

"Oh, yes," said the goat. "I am a very good singer. And I always like to sing the last thing at night before I go to sleep."

Now the wolf thought that this was a very funny goat, so he said, "Brother Goat, sing to me, for I have never heard a goat sing."

So the goat put back his head and called, "B-a-a, b-a-a."

"I think that is very funny," said the wolf. "Is that all that you can sing?"

"Oh, no," said the goat. "I have more to sing."

And the goat put back his head and called, "B-a-a, b-a-a, b-a-a."

The dog heard the goat calling. He ran up the hill as fast as he could go.

The wolf saw the dog coming and he ran away. He did not get a goat to eat that night.

How the Rabbit Fooled the Whale and the Elephant

The whale is the biggest animal in the sea. And the elephant is the biggest animal on land. And one day the elephant and the whale were talking together.

"You are the biggest animal in the sea," said the elephant, "and you can be king of the sea. Now I am the biggest animal on the land. And I can be king over all the animals on the land."

"I think that is just what we should do," said the whale. "You would make a good king on the land and I would make a good king in the sea. Then we could do just as we please."

Now a little rabbit heard the whale and the elephant talking. "Not so fast, Mr. Whale and Mr. Elephant," thought the rabbit. "You are not going to be king over me."

The rabbit ran away and got a big rope, and then he went down to the sea to talk to the whale.

"You are so big," said the rabbit, "and I am so little. Will you please be kind and help me?"

"Yes," said the whale, "I will help you. What do you want me to do?"

"My cow is in the mud and I cannot get her out," said the rabbit. "I have tried and I have tried, but I cannot pull her out."

"How can I pull your cow out of the mud?" asked the whale. "I cannot come up on the land to help you. You know that I cannot live on the land. I have to live in the sea."

"I will put this rope around you," said the rabbit. "Then I will put the rope around my cow. When I call, 'Pull. Pull,' I know that you can pull my cow out of the mud."

"All right," said the whale. "I will help you. "Put the rope around me. Call to me and I will pull. I will get your cow out of the mud."

Then the rabbit ran off to find the elephant.

"Oh, Mr. Elephant," said the rabbit. "You are so big and I am so little. Will you please be kind and help me?"

"Yes," said the elephant. "What do you want me to do?"

"My cow is in the mud and I cannot get her out," said the rabbit. "I have tried and I have tried, but I cannot pull her out."

"How can I pull your cow out of the mud?" asked the elephant.

"Let me put this rope around your trunk. Then I will put the rope around my cow," said the rabbit, "and when I call, you pull and you pull."

"All right," said the elephant. "Put your rope around my trunk. Call to me and then I will pull and pull. I will get your cow out of the mud."

The rabbit put the rope around the elephant's trunk. Then the rabbit called out, "Pull. Pull."

The whale heard. The elephant heard. The whale and the elephant pulled and pulled on the rope.

The whale put his tail down in the sea and he pulled and he pulled. The elephant could not keep his feet under him. He began to fall down. Then he saw that it was the whale in the sea that was pulling him.

The elephant pulled and he pulled. The rope broke. Down went the whale into the sea. And over and over went the elephant.

And after that the whale and the elephant never talked together. The whale did not want to be king in the sea. And the elephant did not want to be a king on the land. And the rabbit laughed and laughed. He had fooled the whale. He had fooled the elephant. And now there was no king over him.

The Jackal and the Camel

There was once a jackal who liked to eat crabs. The crabs lived by the river, and the jackal had eaten all the crabs that he could find on his side of the river.

"I wish that I could swim to the other side of the river," said the jackal. "I know that there are many crabs there."

The jackal wanted to get to the other side of the river, so he went to see the camel.

"I know how you like to eat sugarcane," said the jackal to the camel. "And I know where there is some very good sugarcane."

"It was kind of you to think of me," said the camel. "Tell me where I can find the sugarcane and I will go and get some."

"No," said the jackal, "I cannot tell you where the sugarcane is; I will have to show you where the sugarcane is."

"All right," said the camel. "Show me where the sugarcane is so that I can eat some. You do not know how good sugarcane is."

"I like to eat crabs," said the jackal. "And there are many good crabs on the other side of the river. And much good sugarcane grows on the other side of the river, too."

"I will swim to the other side of the river," said the camel, "and get some of that good sugarcane."

"But I will have to show you where the sugarcane grows," said the jackal. "Now if I could just ride upon your back, we could both get to the other side of the river."

And that is just what they did.

When the camel and the jackal were on the other side of the river, the jackal showed the camel the farmer's sugarcane. Then the jackal ran down to the river to find crabs.

Now the jackal is small and in no time at all he had eaten all the crabs that he could eat. Then he wanted to go back to his house and sleep. But his house was on the other side of the river.

The jackal went back to the camel. The camel was eating the sugarcane. Now the camel is big. He was not full of sugarcane, and so he ate and he ate. But the jackal wanted to get back to his house on the other side of the river.

The jackal started to sing. He ran around and around the sugarcane, singing and singing.

The farmer and his boys heard the singing. They saw the camel eating their sugarcane. They ran after the camel. The camel ran down to the river and there he found the jackal.

"Come," said the camel. "Jump upon my back. We must swim to the other side of the river. The farmer and his boys are after us."

The camel with the jackal on his back started into the water.

The camel said to the jackal, "Why did you start to sing, Jackal? The farmer and his boys came and found me in their sugarcane. Why did you start to sing?"

"Oh," said the jackal," I like crabs very much, and I always sing after I eat crabs." And the jackal laughed and laughed.

When they were out into the river, the camel said to the jackal, "Now, I think that I will have to roll over."

"Oh, don't roll over," said the jackal. "I will go into the water if you roll over. And I cannot swim."

"But I have to roll over," said the camel. "I always have to roll over when I am not full of sugarcane."

"Don't, don't," said the jackal. But the camel rolled over in the water, and the jackal went down into the river.

The Turtle Who Could Not Stop Talking

There was once a big turtle who lived by a river. The turtle talked to the fish in the river. The turtle talked to the birds in the trees. And the turtle talked to the squirrels and the rabbits that played in the grass.

One day two geese flew down to the river. The turtle talked with the geese. He asked them where they lived.

"We live far away," said the geese. "There the water is blue and the trees are always green."

"I would like to see your home," said the turtle. "I get so tired of living by this river all the time."

Soon after, the two geese flew down to the river again. As soon as the turtle saw them, he asked them to tell him more about their home.

"The birds sing in the trees," said the two geese. "And big red and yellow flowers grow all about. Our home is very pretty, but it is very far away."

"I wish that I could see your pretty home," said the turtle. And the turtle talked and talked of how much he wanted to see their home.

Now the two geese liked the turtle very much. They wanted him to see their pretty home. And so one day they came to the turtle and said, "We know how we can take you to our home, but you will have to stop talking."

The turtle only laughed. "Look at my little legs," said the turtle. "I could never walk to your home far away."

A day or two after that the two geese flew back to the river with a long stick. The geese had the stick by the ends.

"Can you hold on to this stick with your mouth?" asked the two geese.

"Yes," said the turtle.

Then the two geese took hold of the ends of the stick. And the turtle took hold of the stick with his mouth. And then the two geese flew away with the turtle.

Some children looked up and saw the two geese carrying the stick. They saw the turtle holding on to the stick. They laughed and laughed.

"Look, look," called the children. "Two geese are carrying a turtle on a stick. We never saw anything so funny. Two geese are flying away with a turtle."

The turtle looked down and saw the children. He heard the children laughing.

As the turtle opened his mouth to say, "Stop laughing. The geese are taking me to their home," he let go of the stick. Down, down, down he went and landed in a lake.

And as the geese flew home, they said, "The turtle could not stop talking, so he will not get to see our beautiful home."

The Bear Says "North"

One day a big, old bear got hold of a bird. He had the bird in his mouth and he thought, "Just see what I have done. I wish everyone in the woods could see me now. They think that I am a funny, old bear. They are always laughing at me. They do not think that I could get hold of a bird like this."

Just then a fox came by. He saw the bear with the bird in his mouth. And the fox thought, "That funny old bear is very pleased that he got hold of a bird. I think that I will fool him."

The fox walked up to the bear and said, "I have been walking in the woods all morning, but I cannot tell from which way the wind is coming. Mr. Bear, which way is the wind coming from?"

The bear said, "Um, um, um," because he wanted the fox to see the bird he had in his mouth.

But the fox said, "Mr. Bear, did you say that the wind is coming from the south?"

"Um, um, um," said the bear, because that was all he could say with the bird in his mouth.

"Oh," said the fox, "You do not think that the wind is coming from the south."

"Um, um, um," said the bear.

"Well," said the fox, "If you do not think the wind is from the south, tell me, Mr. Bear, from which way do you think the wind is coming?"

The bear opened his mouth and said, "North." As soon as the bear opened his mouth, the bird flew away.

The fox laughed and laughed.

"Just look what you made me do," said the bear. "I wanted to show everyone how I had got hold of a bird."

"I did not make you do anything," said the fox.

"You asked me which way the wind is blowing," said the bear. "I opened my mouth and said 'North,' and the bird flew away."

"But why did you open your mouth?" asked the fox.

"You cannot say 'North' if you do not open your mouth," said the bear.

"Well," said the fox. "If I had had a bird in my mouth and you asked me about the wind, I should not have said 'North'."

"What would you have said?" asked the bear.

The fox laughed and laughed.

Then he put his teeth together and said, "East."

The Hare and the Hedgehog

One morning Mr. Hedgehog went for a walk. The sun was out and the birds were singing. Mr. Hedgehog said, "I think that I shall go and see how my cabbages are growing."

Now the cabbages were really Farmer Brown's cabbages, but the hedgehog always thought that the cabbages were his.

At the cabbage field, Mr. Hedgehog saw Mr. Hare. "Good morning, Mr. Hare," said Mr. Hedgehog. "This is a good morning to be walking in the cabbage field."

"A walk in the cabbage field," laughed Mr. Hare. "I do not see how you can walk in the cabbage field with those little duck legs of yours."

"My legs are all right," said Mr. Hedgehog, who could not help it that his legs were little. "And my legs can do anything that your legs can do."

Mr. Hare looked at Mr. Hedgehog's legs and he looked at his own legs. Then he laughed and laughed.

"I will run a race with you," said Mr. Hedgehog. "And if I win, Mr. Hare, you must keep out of my cabbage field."

"I will run a race with you," said Mr. Hare, "and I will win the race, Mr. Hedgehog. Then you will keep out of my cabbage field."

"We shall see about that," said Mr. Hedgehog.

"Shall we run the race right now?" asked Mr. Hare.

"No, No," said Mr. Hedgehog. "I must go home first and get something to eat."

When Mr. Hedgehog got home, he called to his wife, "Come with me, Mrs. Hedgehog, I want you to help me fool that old Hare who said that we walk on 'duck legs'."

And so Mr. Hedgehog and Mrs. Hedgehog walked back to the cabbage field. Mr. Hedgehog said that he was going to run a race with Mr. Hare.

"You can never win the race," said Mrs. Hedgehog.

"I know that I cannot run as fast as Mr. Hare," said Mr. Hedgehog, "but I can get the better of Mr. Hare. With your help I am going to fool him."

"How can I help you win a race?" asked Mrs. Hedgehog. "And how can I help you fool Mr. Hare?"

"The hare will run down one row of cabbages," said Mr. Hedgehog. "And I will run down one row of cabbages. You will be at the end of my row. And when Mr. Hare gets to the end of his row of cabbages, you, my wife, who looks just like me, are to jump up and say, 'Here I am,' and Mr. Hare will think that I have run the race."

Mr. Hedgehog put Mrs. Hedgehog at the end of the row under a big cabbage. And then he walked up the row of cabbages. He found Mr. Hare asleep and he said, "Mr. Hare, it is time that you had a race with me."

The Hare opened his eyes.

"You run down your row of cabbages," said Mr. Hedgehog. "And I will run down my row of cabbages."

The hare said, "One, two, three, and away."

Off ran the hare as fast as he could go. And when he got to the end of his row, up jumped Mrs. Hedgehog.

"Here I am, Mr. Hare," called Mrs. Hedgehog.

"How did you get here before I did?" said Mr. Hare." Let us run this race again."

"All right," said Mrs. Hedgehog.

And so Mr. Hare said again, "One, two, three, and away."

Off ran the Hare as fast as he could go. And when he got to the other end of his row, up jumped Mr. Hedgehog.

"Here I am, Mr. Hare," called Mr. Hedgehog.

"How did you get here before I did?" said Mr. Hare. "I know that I can run faster than you can. Let us run this race again."

"All right," said Mr. Hedgehog. "Let us race as many times as you like. Shall we start?"

The hare was very tired, but he said, "One, two, three, and away."

Off ran the hare as fast as he could go. And when he got to the other end of his row, up jumped Mrs. Hedgehog.

"Here I am," called Mrs. Hedgehog.

"How did you get here before I did," said Mr. Hare. He was so tired that he did not know what to do, but he would not give up. "Let us run this race again."

"All right," said Mrs. Hedgehog.

And so Mr. Hare said again, "One, two, three, and away."

Off ran the hare as fast as he could go. And when he got to the other end of the row, up jumped Mr. Hedgehog.

"Here I am," called Mr. Hedgehog. "I said that I would win the race. And now don't you call me 'duck legs' again. My little legs can do anything your long legs can do."

But Mr. Hare was so tired that he did not say a thing. He just went home and went to sleep again.

Mr. Hedgehog walked down the row of cabbages on his little legs, and when he got to the end of the row, he called, "Come, Mrs. Hedgehog, it is time for us to be going home." And they both laughed and laughed at the way they had fooled Mr. Hare.

The Blind Men and the Elephant

Six blind men sat by the road. And they talked together of this and that. As they sat there talking, the boy who was with them said, "Here comes a man down the road with an elephant. It is a very big elephant. The man must be taking the elephant to the king."

The six blind men called out, "Ask the man with the elephant to stop. We want to find out what an elephant is like."

The boy ran to the man with the elephant and said that the six blind men wanted to find out what an elephant was like. So the man stopped his elephant right in front of the blind men.

The first blind man put his hands on the elephant's side.

"Now I know what an elephant is like," said the first blind man. "An elephant is like a wall."

Another blind man put his hands on the elephant's tusks.

"No, no, no," said this blind man. "An elephant is not like a wall. My hands tell me the elephant is round and hard."

Another blind man put his hands on the elephant's trunk.

"No, no, no," said this blind man. "An elephant is not like a wall. An elephant is not round and hard. An elephant is round and soft like a snake."

"How can you say funny things like that," said the blind man who had put his hands on the elephant's leg. "An elephant is not like a wall. An elephant is not round and hard. An elephant is not round and soft like a snake. Anyone can tell that an elephant is like a tree."

Now the fifth blind man was a big man. And he put out his hands and took hold of the elephant's ear.

"No, no, no," said the fifth blind man. "An elephant is not like a wall. He is not round and hard. He is not round and soft like a snake. He is not like a tree. I have hold of this elephant with my hands and he is like a big fan."

Then the last blind man laughed and laughed. He had hold of the elephant's tail.

"What funny men you are," he said. "And what funny things you say. I know what an elephant is like. An elephant is like a rope. I hold the rope here in my hand."

Then the six blind men sat down by the road again. And they talked and they talked. Each blind man thought he knew what the elephant was like. And as long as they lived, one blind man thought the elephant was like a wall. And one blind man thought the elephant was round and hard. And one blind man thought the elephant was round and soft like a snake. And one blind man thought the elephant was like a tree. And one blind man thought the elephant was like a big fan. And one blind man thought the elephant was like a rope. And each blind man thought that he was right.

The Monkey and the Woman

Once there was a woman who had many banana trees. But the bananas were so high in the trees that she could not pick them.

The woman knew that she would have to get someone to pick her bananas, so she went to the biggest monkey.

"Monkey," she said, "you like bananas very much."

"Yes," said the monkey, "I like bananas very much."

"I will let you pick my bananas. And I will give you half of the bananas."

The biggest monkey picked the bananas. He gave half of the bananas, all the little ones, to the woman. He kept half of the bananas, all the big ones, for himself.

The woman was very angry. "That big monkey played a trick on me," she said. "Now I will play a trick on him."

The woman made a person out of wax. She put a basket in his lap. In the basket she put the biggest bananas she could find.

Soon the biggest monkey came by. He saw the big bananas and wanted one.

"Please give me a banana," said the monkey.

But the person did not say a word.

"Please give me a banana," said the monkey.

But the person did not say a word.

The biggest monkey got angry. He reached for a big banana. His hand got stuck in the wax.

"Let go of my hand," said the monkey. "Let go of my hand."

The wax person did not let go of monkey's hand. So the monkey tried to pull one hand out of the wax while he pushed with the other hand. No good. Now both hands were stuck in the wax.

"Let go of my two hands," said the monkey. "Let go of my hands."

The person did not say a word.

The monkey pushed against the wax person with one foot. His foot stuck in the wax. The monkey pushed against the wax person with the other foot. His other foot stuck in the wax.

The biggest monkey could not move. He called to the other monkeys.

"Come and help me. Come and help me. This person will not let me go."

The other monkeys came. They saw the person made of wax. They saw the biggest monkey stuck in the wax. The monkeys did not know what to do.

Then the littlest monkey said, "Let us call to the sun. The sun will melt the wax."

All the monkeys called to the sun. "Sun, Sun, beautiful Sun. Come and help the biggest monkey."

The sun came. The sun was very hot. The wax began to melt.

Soon the biggest monkey pulled one hand out of the wax. Then he pulled the other hand out of the wax.

The biggest monkey pulled one foot out of the wax. Then he pulled the other foot out of the wax.

The woman saw that the sun had melted the wax.

"I am going away," said the woman to herself. "I am going to grow corn. The monkeys may have all the bananas."

a
about
after
again
against
all
always
am
Ambe
an
and
angry
animal
animals
another
answer
answered
any
anyone
anything
are
around
as
ask
asked
at
ate
away
baa
back
banana
bananas
basket
be
bear
beautiful
because

been
before
began
better
big
biggest
bird
birds
black
blind
blowing
blue
both
bow
bowed
boy
boys
bring
broke
brother
brothers
Brown's
but
by
cabbage
cabbages
call
called
calling
came
camel
can
cane
cannot
carrying
cat
children

come	faster
comes	feet
coming	field
corn	fifth
could	find
cow	first
crabs	fish
day	flew
did	flowers
do	flying
dog	fool
doing	fooled
done	foot
don't	for
door	found
down	fox
duck	friend
each	friends
ear	from
east	front
eat	full
eaten	funny
eating	garden
elephant	gave
elephant's	geese
end	get
ends	gets
every	give
everyone	glad
eyes	go
fall	goat
fan	goats
far	going
farm	good
farmer	got
farmer's	grass
fast	green

grow	into
growing	is
grows	it
had	jackal
half	jump
hand	jumped
hands	just
hard	keep
hare	kept
have	kind
he	king
head	knew
heard	know
hedgehog	knows
hedgehog's	lake
help	land
her	landed
here	lap
herself	last
high	laughed
hill	laughing
hills	leg
him	legs
himself	legs'
his	let
hold	like
holding	liked
home	little
hot	littlest
house	live
how	lived
hump	living
hungry	long
hurt	look
I	looked
if	looking
in	looks

made
make
man
many
may
maybe
me
melt
melted
men
mice
monkey
monkeys
monkey's
more
morning
mouse
mouth
move
Mr.
Mrs.
much
mud
must
my
never
next
night
no
north
nose
not
now
of
off
oh
old

on
once
one
only
open
opened
or
other
our
out
outdone
over
own
person
pick
picked
pig
play
played
please
pleased
pretty
pull
pulled
pulling
pushed
put
rabbit
rabbits
race
Rambe
ran
reached
really
red
ride
right

river
road
roll
rolled
rope
round
row
run
said
sat
saw
say
says
sea
see
seven
she
should
show
showed
side
sing
singer
singing
sit
six
sleep
sleeping
small
smallest
snake
so
soft
some
someone
something
sometimes

soon
south
squirrels
start
started
stick
stop
stopped
stuck
sugarcane
sun
swim
tail
take
taking
talk
talked
talking
tall
teeth
tell
than
thank
that
the
their
them
then
there
they
thing
things
think
thinking
this
those
thought

three
time
times
tired
to
today
together
tonight
too
took
tree
trees
trick
tried
trunk
try
turtle
tusks
two
um
under
up
upon
us
very
walk
walked
walking
wall
want
wanted
was

water
wax
way
we
well
went
were
whale
what
when
where
which
while
who
why
wife
will
win
wind
wish
with
wolf
woman
woods
word
would
yellow
yes
you
your
yours